Obsession with the Dogwood

Obsession with the Dogwood

Jane Blue

ALSO BY JANE BLUE

Poetry Books

The Madeleine Poems
Now That I Am in the Light I See: New Poems
The Persistence of Vision
Blood Moon

Poetry Chapbooks

Sacrament
Turf Daisies and Dandelions

Memoir

My Mother and Amelia Earhart

Obsession with the Dogwood
Copyright © 2018 Jane Blue

Author photo by Peter Rodman
Cover and title page painting by Deborah Ann Dawson

First Flowstone Press Edition • July 2018
ISBN 978-1-945824-17-3

Printed in the United States of America

Flowstone Press
Illinois Valley, OR
www.leftfork.org/flowstone

for Peter and his
decades of patience

Contents

1

Sunday Morning	5
Obsession with the Dogwood	6
Smoke	8
If You Are a Prisoner	9
Hummingbird	10
Frankenstein's Monster Looks Back	11
Snapshots	12
Dinosaur Tail	13
Whirlpool	14
On a Painting by John Meyer	15
The Orient Express	16

2

Curtains	21
Feathers	22
Windows	23
The Woman Who Fed the Doves	24
The Acorn	25
California Bank & Trust	26
Hospital, 8th Floor	27
The Mystery of Animate Beings	28
The Eavesdropper	29
In Defense of Plants	30

3

Excerpt from a Journal	35
Quotations	36
Typist's Notes	37
Who Is the Bear?	38
In the Sandwich Shop	39
The Last Rose of Summer	40
Whale-Watching	41
Emergency Room	42
Dying	43
This is the Place	44
Agapanthus, or Lily of the Nile	45

4

At The Doctor's Office	51
Hummingbird Ghazal	52
Not a Word	53
Pity Us	54
Miracles	55
Sudden Death	56
Warrior Woman	57
The Language of Walking	58
Death Takes a Holiday	59
A Night Out	60

5

Spring and Fall	65
Go With Me, God of the Dogwood	66
A Leaf Drops	67
Roses in March	68
The Man Wearing Towels	69
A Moment in April	70
Ode to a Geranium	71
The Narrow Infinitive of Life	73

6

Ciao	77
Exotic Birds	78
Evolution	79
Ash and Bones	81
Boy with Guitar	82
Geese and the Sun	83
Start with Not Being on Fire	84
November	85
The Last Day of the Year	86
A Cat Sits Under the Moon	87
He and She	88
Acknowledgements	90
About the Author	92

Obsession with the Dogwood

1

Sunday Morning

A great wind shakes the Rose of Sharon.
Then a red squirrel leaps out
and all is still. The tree no longer
laden with its floral display.

It's Fall, the russet leaves of dogwood
bob as in a terrible, Biblical wind.
Until a crow darts out horizontally
as though embarrassed.

Maybe it wasn't a crow.
So many things are fuzzy now
like my father at his typewriter
in a photo from the Thirties.

I know more about the life
of the dogwood.
Most of its leaves are gone or faded now.
Small birds ravish the berries—

You are asleep, and I will be soon.
Then we will get up
and go to lunch.

Obsession with the Dogwood

1.

It is officially Spring. The dogwood
blooming lacy and spindly
in the shade of the plane tree.

Under the plane tree, a flock
of parrot tulips gold-orange
with crenellated petals like wings.

And bright yellow tulips
with black centers like eyelashes.
A cherry tree across the street.

Why do I think of the past?
I don't miss anyone, not badly.
And it was a different place

with elms and blue-eyed forget-
me-nots under an ancient deodar tree.
The generation before me

has faded away, as this season
of flowers will. You must create
the world from nothing yourself.

2.

Every morning I think marriage
an amazing state to be in.
The roses laid out in the window

like a bouquet; the sprays
of white dogwood, pink geraniums
flowing down from a pot, entwined

with red roses. And we are there
with them, silently, two thirds
of our lives together, meshed here.

Separation would tear out
the hearts of those flowers. We
are in our winter now, but here

at the end of winter, the roses,
the dogwood, the geraniums
begin to bloom.

Smoke

Another week has begun
its inevitable climb to the future.

There is the lace of sycamore twigs
beyond the bent pruned rose canes.

I like to look at the smoke that swirls
from the neighbor's chimney, up
into the fog, disappearing
and returning again. Thinking how

I would shyly give my grandmother
little packets of poems, which she
looked at about the way she looked at
the gift mouse in the cat's jaws.

The cat wasn't *her* cat, but the cat
chose my little grandmother: steely-
eyed and corseted, whom the cat knew
was the neediest person in the house.

If You Are a Prisoner

You can make poems from almost anything
as long as you have some bread for the yeast.

What I actually wrote was: "You can make
pruno* from almost anything
as long as you have some bread for the yeast."

If you are a prisoner, or have ever been
in prison, you will understand.

A single brown leaf jutters madly
on a high branch of the sycamore
hanging on for dear life.

Life.

If you are a prisoner, that word—
"life"—is not a hopeful one.

Later another leaf at the very top
of another sycamore, flails like a ragged
Christmas ornament.

Life.

* pruno: homemade prison liquor

Hummingbird

A tiny hummingbird flies into the hibiscus flowers
of the Rose of Sharon, into the darting bees.

I can't see her drink, she is so quick, her
trajectory so wild, slave to the air's movement

invisible to my eye, my heavy, land-tethered
form. A gulp must be less than a drop

but for her it's a whole meal. Her fast-beating heart
is the size of a fingernail's crescent moon.

Her energy the energy of God; she's always busy
in her heaven. Hers seems a hectic life to me.

It is simply life. A flash of color draws her,
a bit of sweetness. And then she must be off!

***

Oh the world is strange and varied.
Who you think you are, and who you think

your parents are, who you think your sisters
and brothers are, who you think

the hummingbird is and what she knows—
that is always fiction.

Frankenstein's Monster Looks Back

We are always seeing, always
discovering
how deceitful memory
mutates into fiction.

When I was a child, I believed
if I had the key I could walk
into a painting
and disappear there.

Big aromatic leaves of nasturtiums
encircled the house and I would
fling open the casements,
lean out and inhale the fragrance.

I never was really young
but I was innocent.

Memory is circular.
You began to call me "Fiend,"
my handsome maker.
I was no longer
what you intended.

I searched and searched
for that child I remembered
seeing my monster reflection
in cottage windows.

All the way out here
in the howling winds
and the icy wastes.

Snapshots

Tulip magnolias brave the cold mornings
bleed into frost. People take pictures of them
budding, satiny, in layers of magenta and cream.

They are like laundry on the bare branches,
freezing and thawing, freezing and thawing.

It's January in California and spring
pops up everywhere: camellias

dropping petals like ragged petticoats
from the laundry line; flowering quince

flaming from unleaved branches spiky
with thorns. Calla lilies poking up their
shafts, ready to unfurl into flowers.

People also like to snap pictures
of the moon. The moon is so close

they feel an intimacy they don't feel with the sun.
The sun turns its fire to us every day.

The moon hides its face, has phases
like we do, pocked as with some human

disease. With zoom lenses they feel
as close to the moon as to their hung laundry.

Dinosaur Tail

The father's cells—his gene pool—
mingle in the mother's womb
and become part of her.

I read this somewhere.

I took only elementary biology
in college. I learned the word
zygote, I learned the word *osmosis*.

This phenomenon, I guess
is a kind of osmosis, cells seeping
across boundaries. I didn't know then
how soon it would happen to me, how
I was on the verge of meeting that man
who would penetrate me so profoundly
that even his genealogy
would become mine.

Kansas, Missouri, Cherokee.

All those lives trailing behind me
like a dinosaur tail, all the way back
to the Jurassic Age. His lives
with each child. A dinosaur tail.

Those feelings, "I know this place,
these people." All those years
of separation cannot diminish:

Kansas, Missouri, Cherokee.

Whirlpool
On a digitally altered photograph by Bill Domenikos

Just like that, you found
yourself in the whirlpool
that sucked the life
from your throat, your heart, leaving
your vision without color.

This picture is so naked
I can barely see anything
except that hole. Your whole past.

Please take that shawl
which you have drawn off
your naked shoulders
and cover your gaping

throat. I don't want to see it.
Please!

The eddy, the glory
hole of your feelings
like some saint, some martyr.

On a Painting by John Meyer

You are leaving me again and again
and again and again and again.

I am on a long train, I'm backed against a wall
in the dining car, empty plates of our dinner

strewn on a table in the diner; I am hunched
over it and you are standing in that place

between cars where it rumbles and rocks
and the cold night air whooshes in

with the odor of the fields. I have been on
this train for a long time, for too long.

Trees blur in the window pane, and grass
and telephone poles, and sometimes

the stucco houses of a small town, and then
the pitch dark of the tunnels where the sound

of the great wheels is magnified by the track,
ka-chink, ka-chink. And the low moan

of the whistle at the front of the train slinking
around a bend. You are turned away from me

and at the same time twisted toward me
in that pneumatic space between cars.

I'm looking at you with my mind's eye between
now and then. Again and again and again.

The Orient Express

A wall of windows, a door of shadows
all around me where I slept as a child.

Does time fly, or does it
circle the earth like a train? Like
the Orient Express boring down into Russia.

Embrace this moment. Look around.
Feel the cool morning air.

My mother rode that train once
blithely smuggling in rubles.

Does time fly in a straight line? Not even
the birds, except perhaps occasionally a crow.
Not even a plane.

There is a turbulence in the layers of air.
Watch a bird or a butterfly use it.

Justin next door is drumming again, a dog
sings. When the time comes, Justin,
drum me out, drum me home.

2

Curtains

> "Let us learn to live swaying
> As in a rocking boat on the sea."
> —Friedrich Holderlin, trans. Robert Bly

The four of us walk in cold light rain—
four umbrellas: blue, blue, rose and beige.
The rose and the beige twirl and bow
at the entrance of the restaurant like a French film.

Then the pale sun of winter curls in, around
and under the canvas curtains
that hang halfway down mullioned
double-paned windows. They sag in places
from the weight of ticking, stitches ripped,
a panel undone. Someone begins a conversation
about the Resurrection.

The single curtain with its folded double
torn away from it, distorts the shadows behind it,
thickening them. The curtain is less opaque
than the others, off-center, that is, *eccentric*.

A fair young woman with crimped golden hair
sits straight up, alone at a table by the window.
She resembles the Flemish virgin of von Cleef's
"Annunciation" reduced on a Christmas card.

A line came to me this morning
from the unraveling edges of sleep: "The lonely,
isolated eyes of God."
He peeks through the curtains and sees us laughing.

Feathers
after Stanley Plumly

A new pillow throws feathers through the house
like a trail of ducklings, or goslings, or more likely
a hen's chicks, the plucked down white as snow
turning yellow being trod on, like snow. Somehow
they remind me of birth, the blank slate of it.

Some say they have been born again in the Lord,
the past wiped away. What if we all could be born anew?
Memories become crystallized and then you remember
the line said about it, or a photograph, sepia, that you
tint with your brain. Some say they can remember

that rush into the world, the escape from the womb.
I was told, "You slipped out like a watermelon seed,"
the second twin, the smaller, the one who often
does not survive, lonely in the incubator (I'm sure
I remember the loneliness) where the other was not.

Our mother, depleted, exhausted, could not nurse.
The other's formula richer, yet she bawled and bawled
with hunger, greedily emptying her bottle. Our mother
snatched mine, half full, and plunged it into the other's
gaping mouth. I happily, sleepily, relinquished it.

Our mother felt guilty, but I did not. We were so
close in the womb, although there were eight
minutes between us, and two placentas. This
is the story we were told. That I slipped out silently
while my mother slept—and my sister wept.

Windows

> "All the windows were open in her heart."
> —D.R. Wagner

Means to look out on the whole wide world.
To escape down the sidewalk, down the road.

Silent, extra eyes. Silent swinging outward limbs.
Out when you are in. In, intimate, when you are out.

In the cold, in the heat. Sometimes mullioned like a cage.
Mysterious, foreign in photographs from abroad.

Flower boxes, geraniums spilling over
Plastered walls, a woman leaning out, smiling.

Open windows, sheer gauze curtains billowing.
Open like her heart. Or shuttered like a closed face.

Shutters painted cerulean or vermillion, flung open.
A woman turning away. A woman flirting.

A hummingbird flickering in the glass, yellow-breasted.
A sparrow that hovers, hummingbird-like.

A reflection in the window. You. In the roses, in the street.
Disembodied. A spirit. The spirit that sways the rose.

The wind blowing rain sideways. A pink bud of rose.
Pushing high toward winter sun. In the wrong season.

The pink rose that will soon be pruned.
That will come back in spring.

The Woman Who Fed the Doves

Short and compactly Sicilian
she was the pastor's mother—a priest—

her only child; a son. She started her car
every morning, put it in gear, gunned it

in a semi-circle from curb to curb
until one day she plowed across the street

into camellias and stucco down to the mesh.
Someone called police; the priest came

flapping his pudgy hands. She fed mourning
doves in her back yard, a grey cloud

of thousands and thousands of them,
sated, leaving. Always some drama.

She would stand on the sidewalk, aiming
the Evil Eye—*Il Malocchio*—

through a living room window.
I used to hear the call and response

of doves softly echoing across treetops.
The priest finally put his mother in a place

where she died, and the doves went away.
Now all I hear is the raucous cawing of crows.

As though they've won.

The Acorn

A large talkative man wearing stonewashed
blue jeans, one leg pulled up
and tied around a stump, burst
out of a drizzly morning.

A thin silent woman followed
and went immediately to the counter.

He turned to me and said
"Have you ever seen an acorn this big?"
thrusting it between his thumb and forefinger.
Shyly, I felt it, gritty
from the soil under an oak
that I imagined magnificent, dropping
hundreds of acorns, perhaps spreading
over a vacant lot in the city, squirrels
scrambling, a sign of a cold winter to come.
A humble acorn, the obvious little acorn cap
on top of a polished eyeless face.

The man clanked down hard into a metal chair
waiting for the almost invisible woman.
"I like the little things, I guess," he sighed.
Then she came and nodded to him
and they left out into a fine mist.
I watched him swing his truncated leg
over a bicycle, pushing with his good one,
the thin woman walking beside him.

California Bank & Trust

An azure sky, not a cloud anywhere,
yet it is bitter, bitter
to think of the crumpled people beneath it
huddled in camps like Canada geese,
wearing their odd hand-me down clothes.

Here in the shade
of the California Bank & Trust
moss spreads between bonsai.
There is an open bottle of malt liquor
not even emptied where a man
fell into oblivion

after the periscope of his
hypervigilance swiveled as he sat
splayed, begging for change
from people exiting the bank. The Bank

and Trust. I am only imagining him there,
feeling the visceral
pang you get
when the one you love lies bleeding.

Hospital, 8th Floor

She comes in suffering, keening,
huffing and sobbing, won't
lie down docile
but crouches on old
hospital linoleum rocking
barefoot in an ancient
African way, and her cousin
watches, feeling
her pain. The cousin
waits on the bed all night;
until near dawn when the woman
in pain lies flat in the bed
and sleeps—then she and her cousin
leave back to the streets
from where they have come.

In the morning a crow, quiet
and oblivious, rides air
outside the window
from somewhere above the eighth floor
an escalator
made of down draft that I would
plummet, gravity-bound. Its goal
unlike my father, jumping from his hotel
on the same length of sky, is life, food
it sharp-eyed sees, rodent
in its talons, or dove-egg in its beak.

The Mystery of Animate Beings

Two women are studying the Bible
at a black table by the window
in the new café with sunny yellow walls.
"Do not be afraid," Jesus says to his disciples.
I'm not afraid for myself, but for the world.
Jesus! People are fighting in your name.
A little girl hangs onto the counter and wails:
"No!" In all languages "No!" comes
roaring out of the ego at two. *Nein! Nyet!
Non! ¡No!* And then "I don't want to!"
excruciatingly well-enunciated. The mother
is tired, propping herself up with espresso.
As they leave, I see a bundled infant
in the crook of her left arm. The toddler
is on her own, scuffing her shoes, whimpering.
A crow flies by the window, wings swept back
like a stealth bomber. I wish I didn't know
that metaphor: stealth bomber. I also
don't like to say "it" for animate beings,
but it's hard to tell gender in crows. I think
stereotypically of all crows as masculine,
thieves and connivers. Argumentative
as they are, I've never seen one with a rifle.
Their wars are confined to verbal assaults
like the little girl in her sweet pink clothes.
The mother, bless her, doesn't retaliate,
slap or raise her voice. I walk out after them
and look at the flowers and the sky.

The Eavesdropper
found in a journal, April 2, 2008

The smell of orange rind under my fingernails,
the taste of strawberries, destroyed
still life on a black saucer. I ate all the grapes.
Some people are talkers, some are writers.
A murderer left detailed notes of his crime.
He was, unfortunately, a writer. His words
condemned him. Some think
it's dangerous to commit anything to paper.
Words can't capture an accent. I'm eavesdropping
on a Texan storyteller. "The cat
was right behind me." A cougar, a puma,
or her own housecat? The hostage-taker
of the storyteller. Words. I once wrote
that I wanted fewer of them. They fill up the world.
Rumors of war and celebrity gossip.
I am not a good storyteller, nor a good
joke teller. A woman from Ukraine finishes
my joke: What do you call someone who speaks
two languages? Bilingual.
What do you call someone who speaks one?
American.

In Defense of Plants

Carrots, with the golden rings of trees inside,
jump off the cutting board when you chop them.
Even grass is scythed or pulled out of the earth
like hair, and nuts, seemingly given so freely
by the trees, must be prised open like clams,
the meat (that is what we call it) splayed out
like a mammalian brain in the shell of its skull.
Soy beans are pressed through screens
until they are lifeless as smooth cubed stones,
then molded and colored to look like pork or beef
(the message: you can't do without it).
Sprouted beans thread out into filaments
like antennae. You might as well be eating insects.
The emptied sprouts open like mouths
reminiscent of carnivorous plants. If plants
eat meat, why shouldn't we? Sadly, there may
not be such a thing as nonviolence. The onions
with their souls exposed, how I weep with them.

3

Excerpt from a Journal

Everything is awakening:
the feathery leaves of elms.
And I shall too.

Birds in conversation, then
they stop as if aware
of being overheard. Rain flows
down the kitchen window
like tears down a face. All lives

have tears, except the lives
of those who cannot spill that
little catharsis. They suffer so—
a permanent drought in their lives.

The incandescent blossoms
of dogwood, whiter than snow
hang on in the rain.
In the distance, the hoot
of a train passing through.

Quotations

Updike wrote: "Yet even in the dead of winter
the sere twigs prepare their dull buds."

Rain gurgles incessantly like the stream
under our love-nest in Vermont.

In Milan cars moved like a line of horses
out of their racing stalls. We are

at an intersection, my sister and I. She says,
"Let's cross down there—at the light."

I remember when she ate a raw onion
like an apple and fell into the lake.

You, my impish love, say: "They should put
little lumps of asphalt all over the road like acne."

A tour bus with blind eyes goes by the cafe.
They can see out but we can't see in.

Typist's Notes

Morning sunlight pokes through the slats
of the jalousies and falls on the floor in scraps
like paper. I try to pick it up, but I can't.

They picked her off the tracks, the woman
who threw herself under a train, surviving
with every limb severed. She rolled down
the church aisle in her wheelchair, singing
Glory Hallelujah, and the congregation
answered, Glory, Hallelujah!

A man tried to hang himself
but it didn't work, he was found
with a broken larynx,
coming to therapy to regain speech,
what he had to say missing from the record.

Another man drank lye, an agonizing way to go;
he woke sicker than he'd ever been,
surprised, and blind. He learned
to tap a white cane and walk among the sighted,
half ghost. There is a desire
beyond conscious desire, of life itself to live.

It is hard to die. The day progresses. A red rose
catches the late-day sun and glows
through the window like a neon light, saying "Stop!"
the color of the blood of all the girls
who saw at their wrists, secretly hoping
they will wake saved, and most of the time they will.

Who Is the Bear?

He has grown too menacing for friendship.
He watches men in the woods
and women in their pantries.
He has no way to speak to them
but he wants something.
He lumbers into their houses. He tries
out a church, breaking the handle from
the church hall door. He goes to a table
and eats 22 jars of peanut butter
to be packed off to the poor. He is the poor.
The lids fall apart in his claws. He has
no idea how strong he is. He sniffs
and slurps. No one is there to see
his bad manners. He walks to the kitchen
and opens the refrigerator the usual way,
pushing the handle, releasing the sweet
odor of oranges. He punctures
a dozen cans of concentrate, licking
the cardboard, as easy for him
as raking a hive of honey. He swipes
a few sweet rolls, then leaves,
damaging little except his own wild
heart. The pastor asks his flock to pray
for the bear. Pray for him to stop ravishing
their homes, be caught and returned
to a paradise that no longer exists.
The wilderness has abandoned the bear.
He is alone and hungry.
He no longer knows what he is hungry for.

In the Sandwich Shop

Death has slipped in before us
into the sandwich shop. Death
in a black hooded sweatshirt.
Skinny Death. Death sprawls
on the glass counter, over the lettuce
and tomatoes, his jeans
barely held up on his hips. He keeps
falling asleep, then waking
to choose meat for his sandwich,
shaking his head, no, no. No
to the vegetables. The counter server
looks startled and impatient
as any of us are in the face of Death.
Addicted Death, withdrawing
from the obsession, tired
of taking so many souls. Death
moves down to the cash register
and pays the price. He manages
to balance a soda and stumble
to a table; slumped in a chair
he falls asleep and a bit of dark face
peeks from behind the hood. Death
wakes twice, sobbing in big gulps
and never touches his food.

The Last Rose of Summer

Imagine yourself as an opera singer
breathing song,
tripping up and down the scales
every day, athletic, like running
up and down staircases for exercise,
learning the words for love
in Italian, French, German, Russian:
whatever you're asked for,
spewing syllables as loudly as you can,
because you mean them—
even the words for hate, and all
the other passions: sorrow,
jealousy, anger. You are
larger than life; it must be a little
like blowing glass, your lungs a bellows
in a hot furnace, as exhausting
and exhilarating as sex;
even in those heavy, brocaded clothes
you are naked, you lie down on the floor,
you swoon off the bed and the bell
of your voice becomes
a body all its own; right now
the soprano is soaring into the aria,
"Letze Rose," from *Martha*,
and suddenly I am crying, lifted
on those notes that I could never reach—
Oh, but if I could! My lungs
and diaphragm pumping and expanding
I would live
forever.

Whale-Watching

My mother went down to Mexico
to watch the mother whales calve.

I don't know what to feel.

Down to San Ignacio Lagoon
where the whales trek
such a long way
for privacy, I would think,
for the warm, amniotic waters.

They are said to be friendly.
I don't know what whales feel.

You felt awe, and maybe
an affinity. The whales sing.

But are they singing for you?

I want to say,
Leave them alone, Mother.
Leave them alone.

Emergency Room

Goodbye to the black man in chains
returning to the concrete floor
of his prison cell.

Where he had a seizure this morning
and opened a gash in his forehead
like a cabbage.

Gray-suited and stoic, the guards
handcuff him, surround him
and shuffle him out.

He says, I hope they cleaned up
the blood from my cell.

A cabbage doesn't bleed red blood
like everyone
who is human.

Dying

When the cat was dying, she shrieked
from the dark hallway, lifting her head

and dragging her failed haunches toward,
perhaps, the light. He went to her

and picked her up, carrying her to the sofa
and setting her on his lap, near the window

where she had liked to sit on the sill
and watch the day go by. She kept slipping

to the floor and he kept picking her up again.
Then she arched her back, staring

at something far off, and hissed
and raised one paw, claws extended, cuffing

death coming through the autumn window;
and then it was over, and then he cried.

This is the Place

Where the mummified anomalies were stored.
Where anomalies in chloroform were stored.

My God! It was here in the hospital basement.
Where the mummified anomalies were stored.

Where—what were they—tiny conjoined twins?
Where—what were they—misshapen embryos?

Where then I worked in the rooms upstairs.
Where I typed what the doctors dictated.

Where someone took me down to the basement.
Where they showed me anomalies in glass jars.

Where anomalies were arrayed on wooden shelves.
Where rows and rows of them were arrayed.

Where nurses and doctors are now, out there.
Where the saving machines hem and haw.

Where I lie in a cubicle, a transom for light.
Where we're all arrayed in a circle of cubicles.

Where nurses and doctors sit and stand, out there.
Where the saving machines hem and haw.

Agapanthus, or Lily of the Nile

This is a meditation on death.

It starts with the agapanthus, a short
agapanthus tucked under a tall agapanthus:
perhaps cousins of the same color,
perhaps a different species. Both a tropical
azure blue.

Wait, death will come, but first the one flower
of the short agapanthus hatches like a robin chick,
pecking at its green pod, which hangs on
like a shard of eggshell or the egg tooth. I can
almost hear it chirping.

We saw doves lay eggs in a basket on the porch,
the mother and father both sitting on them
and hatching them. None of the hatchlings survived.

The individual spikes of flowers of the tall agapanthus
at first almost glow, but in only a few weeks
they droop and fade; and the same
with the short agapanthus.

And a butterfly sits in the tall agapanthus,
let's say it's a Monarch although it could be
the smaller, duller Viceroy.

But let's say it's a Monarch, king of butterflies.
It twitches its wings, then folds them so that the butterfly
is just a line barely seen while it sips agapanthus nectar.
Then it opens its showy wings and lifts high
into the realm of the sky.

I have seen crowds of migrating Monarchs cling to eucalyptus,
a brilliant orange and black display in Monterey,
and some dropped laconically to the ground for a sip of dew.

And some hadn't enough energy to rise back up.
This is a meditation on death.

There are four stages to the butterfly's development
and each one is a new life, a resurrection of sorts.
And each life is very short, as all life is short.
Even ours. It is all relative.

And then, if the butterfly makes it through its four lives
it mates and dies. And the eggs hatch. And the cycle
begins again.

This is a meditation on death.

4

At The Doctor's Office

1

Through a second floor picture window
I'm eye level with the crown
of a magnolia, the first blooms of summer
that start at the top, creamy cups held
in sleek green leaves with their
suede undersides and I realize
I am alone.

2

Another day, outside, under the row
of magnolias on the street
someone has pulled out miniature
agapanthus from the planter bed,
strewn the little onion bulbs
on the sidewalk to be trampled. I think
a child jumped for the fine sky-blue
flowers. Children like to leap for flowers.

3

Once I saw a very small girl bobbing
in my window, appearing
and disappearing up and into
the dogwood tree, until her vague
father ushered her on, white petals
littering the lawn. She wanted
only a handful of stars.

Hummingbird Ghazal

Where a sliver of moon shone just before dawn
now the sun stands dominating the sky.

A hummingbird hovers at the bright
kitchen window, knocking at reflections.

Sometimes the long dead or the silent
absent take up all the space in the house.

A scavenger, bicycle-laden, rifles through
the garbage can, wearing an allergy mask.

I like to hear crickets singing in the night.
They remind me that humans don't rule the world.

And Gene said with a gesture as he left,
"This is all a dream you know."

Not a Word

How do I counter, peacefully, injustice?

*

In this heat the silence of crows, sycamores
still, dull and apathetic.

*

The Jehovah's Witness quotes James:
"...understand this: Everyone
should be quick to listen, slow to speak
and slow to anger."

*

Garbage pickup day.
Green and blue bins soldiering on.
I am grateful
for those who take our garbage away.

*

Eight a.m., but really it's seven.
How do you save daylight? In a jar?
Dawn is dawn. I look at the clock.
I look at the sky, like a farmer, or a bird.

*

At lunch, a woman, I think she's Chinese,
straight-backed alone in a booth, meditates.
Opens her eyes, and smiles right into mine
like a goddess. Not a word passes between us.

Pity Us
> ("Pity us...Pity us All")
> —Elizabeth Strout

A strong sweet smell pushed into the place.
My back was to the door. I whispered:
"What is that, cologne? A man's cologne?"
You grimaced and through clenched teeth answered:
"Unwashed body."

The odor hung suspended like a gauzy curtain.
Finally, I twisted in my chair and got a look for myself—
a small figure stooped by the straws and the napkins.
His face a bitter chocolate, rags obscuring him.

Yes, rags. Not tan, not khaki, not brown,
not grey, but all of those. A no-color.

You told me he had bought some bottled juice.
He seemed to disappear in the glass of the door.
The curtain sagged, but did not dissipate.

The counter girl on break at a table next to a window
looked to the one working across the room
and a tension rustled out, but the odor remained.
Still sweet to me, not the sour stench of the unwashed.

I read the story of a nurse who could go into a room
and smell "a sickly sweet smell," and within a week
that patient would be dead. No one else could detect it.

The odor of death, the odor of roses that is said
to have surrounded a saint on her deathbed.

Pity us...

>   *Pity us all.*

Miracles
for Annie

The benevolent dictator of the sun
rises once more this morning.

Sylvia is reading about our Lady of Lourdes,
a "beautiful lady" who appeared
to 14-year-old Bernadette, by a spring
in the French Pyrenees.

Bernadette dug in the waters of the spring
at the lady's direction, and drank,
and something was healed in the child.

At the end of the day, when the sun
disappears for awhile, as the lady did,
there is a death. There is no miracle.

Annie did not believe in miracles.
She believed she'd go into the ground
and crumble into the soil, and that
would be that.

But a light winks out in the universe
when someone dies, and you feel suddenly
so alive, with the evening sun
glinting in the green, green trees
and a sweet breeze blowing
in the white, white roses.

Sudden Death

      "What they call dying/ is merely the last pain."
           —Ambrose Bierce

It is morning. One red rose among many
glows in the porch's vine as with internal light.
While beyond, in the lawn, white heads

of flowering clover pop out. You can
mow them down but they will rise again.
They remind me of the heartland's prairie

where a field mouse scurries for food
and is swooped down upon and quickly clutched
in the talons of a red-tailed hawk.

She has never in her life flown before, unsure
of the sensation, the vastness, the blueness.
But since birth she has heard tales

of the ominous shadow of wings. Anyway,
she's probably dead from fright even before
the terrible jaws tear into her grey hide.

Warrior Woman

A little Chinese girl sits up on the divider
between tables at McDonald's, like a statue
of a warrior woman. She is wearing a short
pink-patterned dress and blue tights, staring
out the window. Her father, in the booth below,
ignores her as if she isn't even there. Glittery
pink ballet flats graze the benches on either
side of her as her father talk-talks to his friend
across the table, the paper cups of coffee
growing cold. I will call her Susie. Susie
lies back and slips and slides across
McDonald's fake wood slat, unthinkingly.
You know what she is doing even though she
doesn't, exactly. Oh!

Leave this beautiful bored child comforting
herself. This poem, now, is not about her,
she is not Susie, you don't know her at all.
This poem is about you, the deep
embedded loneliness that's always been there
and is now backing out like a fat tick
from your soft flesh, a match lit to it by the doctor.

And the doctor, surprisingly, is you.

The Language of Walking

She walks straight and tall, chest
thrust out, back slightly tilted.

She would bend over backwards for you.

A woman can easily balance the moon on her head.

Roofers are walking on a sloped roof,
jumping from peak to peak, their day-glo
vests and hard hats going with them,
appearing and disappearing
as though they are swinging from trees.

On this day which is not yet Walpurgisnacht,
is not yet Beltane.

Everyone, I think, is scarred.

Death Takes a Holiday

Instead of a ghost they have hung
an effigy of death in the doorway.
His cowled and grinning skeleton face

slues around under the eaves like
the lynched from a tree, sailing out
on October wind that scatters dry leaves.

His arms are held out like the crucified.
His robes are black, his bones are white
and he is thin. He is so thin, he's

transparent. He revolves toward the house,
the sun piercing his robe; he revolves
toward the street, blessing the north,

the south, the east and the west.
"Come, come, you all must come
some day." But he is just tissue paper!

Death is just tissue paper! The children
scamper in and out of the house
ignoring him. They are not afraid of Death.

A Night Out

The sky is a lovely dark blue tonight,
the moon against it ivory
and almost full.

We are at a Japanese restaurant.
A blind couple comes in,
tap-tapping with their canes,
trying to find the door.

The father lugs a large child—
large like the father; if the father fell
he would be like a redwood
crashing down in the forest.

A child seat
is brought to the table. The child
can see. The mother can see
but not much. The father
sits next to the little boy,
touches him like braille.

The mother slides onto the bench
across from them, holds the menu
close to her face, smiles
at the child and mugs at him.

The father keeps putting his hands
on the child, to make sure
he is still there, still safe.

When we leave, I think
the sun is always there, even
at night, beyond the dark blue sky.

5

Spring and Fall

The past roars back in a terrible wind
dropping its debris, like the pungent fruit

from a row of apricot trees in that rented house
on a hill where my daughter learned to walk.

The grape harvest ended early this year.
Peach harvests small, apples too, and plums.

Winter barely crept in with little rain. Fruit
likes its feet to stand in the cold. These times

will be seen as an epoch, when earth warmed
and seas rose. There was enormous wealth

and enormous poverty, crumbling borders,
too many people. Our lives are small,

our generation will pass away and be
the subject of history and myth.

It's a Sunday morning in October,
dogwood leaves flying like bright birds.

And the homeless stand under awnings
of closed shops in the rain.

Go With Me, God of the Dogwood

Wind howled the rain sideways, horizontal
when I was young. My father

was gone. I walked, head bowed
into the wind.

Oh the elements when you are a child!
How you love them.

Go with me, god of the dogwood
and god of the rose.

My mother
pulled aside the homespun curtains

and showed me the Milky Way
like a storm against the sky.

Go with me, god of the dogwood
and god of the rose.

A Leaf Drops
for Eric Weaver

The rose vine after pruning
shoots up every day
like an animal, like a rooster
strutting in the morning breeze
after a night of rain.

Like a rare breed of rooster
with wattle and crest, it will grow
to the roof, the gutters, above the eaves.
Put up a wall of crimson roses,
yellow stamens at each center.

A dry leaf swirls slowly to the ground
and disappears.
And we are left here, disbelieving.
And the lilies and daffodils push up
out of their crumpled bulbs.

Which is the body and which is the soul?

The tulips, the mass of daisies
in the lawn.
And there is the sudden realization
that it is spring.

Roses in March

It's misty this morning, dark and wet
like the womb. I peek through
the rose vine, pruned in January, now
wallowing in its new bronze leaves,
the tips pushing, fanning out. I think they
don't remember a life before pruning.

Roses are everywhere now, red, pink,
white, yellow. Vines that sprawl
over porches and climb to the rooftop.
Bushes pruned into trees, tottering
on one leg mired in the lawn. Thorny
in mulched circular gardens or bordering
the property line; mixed with azaleas
and rhododendrons or majestically
alone. Showy and perfumed, or
small, many-eyed, like those in the wild.

Paul's Scarlet grew on a low fence
between the yards of my childhood,
my father's name that my grandmother
forbade us to speak. Look into the past
and it changes, slippery with ghosts
as more of those that you thought
you knew fade into a phantom horde
and those left behind spill their secrets.

The Man Wearing Towels
    "Look for me in others." —Anon.

He wore terry-cloth bath towels
around his waist, orange, green and purple,
a woman's black velvet jacket
strewn with tiny flowers, and his big feet
were bare. We were a mile from home
not an exotic country. Or was it?
He was in line, mute, unbudgeable.
I wanted to pass by him and find a table.
Please? I'm going to have to step on your foot.
He looked down, dumbfounded.
Concentrated on some coins in his hand.
I got by him finally. He was two cents short
and someone fronted it. Later I saw him
walk out the door, towels, flowers,
hot coffee clutched tight, going
to whatever country he lived in.

A Moment in April

A cat sits on a piece of cardboard,
collapsed box, in sun and shadow.

Sun and shadow, sun and shadow:
that is life. The cat holds tomorrow

in its paws. Loam is piled in the street
and spread across a garden in the making;

bricks line up in the process
of being laid for a walkway; a wooden box

on the driveway, and draped tarps.
From here it looks like an artist's studio.

A baby dove scratches in the gutter.
I'm not sure it can fly. The cat

has disappeared. Has it eaten the dove?
No! It did! It flew! Up into the plane tree.

Up to the nest. So many sweet smells
on the air. So many different bird calls.

Ode to a Geranium

A pink geranium pokes out into sunlight
from its hanging basket.

Some grow wild.
Some climb, some sit decorously in pots.

A hummingbird swoops
black, back-lit in the window.

No, it's too big, it's a cedar waxwing.
My perception, skewed.

Intrepid.

fearless; adventurous.

Like Mia, one year old, walking
into the backyard while all of us
are in the front
ogling the geranium.

Picks up a fallen nectarine and devours it.

The way a geranium catches the light of sunrise
until it glows.

The past and the imagined present
pour in this window thick as honey.
You've never kept bees.

But you know they sting and buzz
much like the past.

You wear a mask, you're clothed in canvas.
With gloved hand you pull out the waxy honeycombs.

Can you do it?

Someone walks away in a violet mist.

The Narrow Infinitive of Life

To be.

One bloom of the old red rose vine
looks like a crimson-winged butterfly.
Perhaps that red is poisonous
like some butterfly wings
that keep predatory birds away.

Sometimes I want to strip
the house of everything, of all memories,
but even the bare floors pull me
into the cavernous past.

***

Let me tell you a story:

A woman stepped down the back steps
of her house, into the empty yard

and was amazed by the sky.

It had been a long time.
Someone mowed once a week
but there were no shrubs,
no flowers around the perimeter.
She was simply

amazed by the sky, the azure of it,
the boats of clouds sailing
in that inverted sea.

6

Ciao

> "...even the air smelled like sexual ecstasy.
> Mosses and ferns were releasing their spores
> into the air."
> —Barbara Kingsolver

The roses and orange blossoms are almost
too overwhelming.

A man says, "Ciao," to his lover, my neighbor.
The curtness of it so intimate.

Sparrows gabble in the green, green trees,
recently bare. A breeze

has laid dogwood flowers on the lawn
like a mirror, or a lake.

A chainsaw whines, and children call
in the same timbre.

Her Japanese maple has just turned
lacy and crimson. His car door slams.

The birds are the loudest things around,
insistent at measured intervals.

People get in their cars and trucks
to go and find nature. An alarm beeps.

A door opens and shuts, a car starts.
My neighbor leaves; she's on her phone.

Exotic Birds

My grandmother said the world
was going to Hell in a handbasket.

It still tilts that way.

Yet the dogwood bronzes
at the edge of paling leaves.
White roses blowse and climb the sky
like exotic birds.

I never believed in Hell.
I believed in white roses and exotic birds.
Believed that my mother, divorced, lapsed
Catholic was never going there.

The nuns reserved Hell for girls
who made out in cars, the cars wrecked,
the girls dying unshriven.

I miss those nuns in flowing black habits,
white wimples, coifs, bibs
like exotic birds.
Young or old, we didn't know the color
of their hair.

Evolution

1

It began with water
the primordial sea

but where did whoever made it
find the water?

Microorganisms somehow
slowly
grew gills and little stubs of legs
and eyes
as the water receded

and voilà!
there was soil
a border between earth and sea.

2

Such a parade on the sidewalk
this morning! A woman
with dark hair piled like a nest
or perhaps
a water container.
Then a blonde
with hair similarly arranged.
Then Justin with his black beard
which could also be a nest
and Kate trailing behind
her hair long and loose, the blonde
grown out of it.

Like magic
they disappear
behind the screen
of the climbing rose vines.

Ash and Bones

Cedar waxwings, black and quick
strip red berries from the dogwood.
I see in my mind's eye the places
that I used to live, now "ash and bones."
The way a geranium catches light
from the east until it glows like fire.
Like fire galed in from eastern hills.
The house in Santa Rosa where
a rose climbed an apple tree, I nursed
a child and grieved a death. Later
fire leered over Sonoma Mountain.
So much fire in my life, the first
a toy box in which I hid my burning
panda, warming him too much
at the heat lamp, and my grandmother,
so tiny and old, smelling the smoke
picked up the box my mother and father
had made, carried it to her bedroom,
pushed it out the window to bare earth
in the lot next door where she
sometimes dropped hollyhock seeds.
The fire of first love which faded
in a Napa suburb with the sameness
of houses and tricycles and Ford
station wagons. I nursed a child there
too, my last, and vowed to have
no more. we walked out into the country,
the baby in his stroller, and talked
and talked to the baby, looked at sheep
scratching their backs on a sagging fence,
rubbing wool off in tufts on the rusted
and knotted barbs of the wire.

Boy with Guitar

There is always the boy with a guitar.

The one who hates the confines of school.

The boy with perfect pitch. Unable
to take piano lessons,
to join the school orchestra.

The minutest shift to sharp or flat
hurts physically.

More than a father's beatings
or a mother's screams.

The boy who can't learn to read music,
the melody crystal in his mind,
the rhythm's strum.

The melody, not the symbol.

He's the dreamy one, the sullen one.

Always on his mother's mind.
The broken one she loves best.

In Japan, they patch cracks in pottery
with gold.

Geese and the Sun

1.
Geese gabbled, got his attention.

Fleeing toward the east in the glare.
The same gray-white color as the sky.

So high, they were like Icaruses,
thousands of them, pulled into the sun.

He could hear them not see them.
Except by the flash of sun on a wing.

He came inside, raising his arms.
Flashing his eyes, and I thought

he would rise and fly away.

2.
Think of the sun, how it rises
every morning even though unseen.

High above clouds and rain.
And there is light. Light on suburbs

and light on farms. You can see
the outlines of houses, of elms
and sycamores, ash and oak.

Cottonwood by the river.
And the moon, pockmarked

reflective, rises in its phases
quietly governs the tides

So we do not fly away.

Start with Not Being on Fire

I am like a stunned bird flown into a window.
And they say, Look, it's breathing.

Huge prehistoric monsters—trucks—
roam the street with a high-pitched warning.

Men speaking Spanish walk beside them.
They wear green and yellow Day-Glo vests.

These denote rank. They wear them over
khaki pants which make their legs look naked.

They jump in and out of trenches
the beasts have clawed out of the street.

With only their torsos showing the men lay
blue pipes, for water, and meters. Sometimes

the house and my chair, with me in it
are lifted up and put down again with a shake

and a thud. I read somewhere, "If you can't
think of anything to be grateful for, start

with not being on fire and work up from there."
At the workday's end, the bird flaps its wings

rises on an updraft, and flies away.

November

Trees have no politics. They shrug off
green and take on crimson and russet.
At the clinic a family rushes to the elevator
from the parking lot. Daddy
pushing Mommy in a wheelchair.
"Daddy, you're so big!" says the little girl
as they all sidle into the elevator going
down. "Daddy will always be big,"
I pipe up. Why? I haven't seen Daddy
since I was three. Outside on the street,
liquidambar and Chinese pistache
and the translucent egg-yolk yellow
of the gingkoes. The family comes
straight in, facing us, Mommy
sits holding her prosthetics on her lap,
three limbs amputated, smooth
and bare as leafless trees, healed stumps
at the joints—the elbows and knees.
When the elevator lands, Daddy
sends the wheelchair fast, through a patio
lined with Bartlett pear trees, the children
scampering alongside.

I stand in their wake and weep.

The Last Day of the Year

A dog barks, a weeping, a roar, a yowl.
It pierces, knifelike, continuously.
I feel it, more than hear it, quivering
under my breastbone. Will the new year
never come? And will we both be new, time
turned upside down, and the dog
will be new, will be loved, will not
cry, or yowl, or roar, not be left alone.

Rains bring ants up from the cellar
confused, disorganized, one at a time.
Without the others they are nothing
and I crush one and then another
under my thumb. Then fog rises
from cold, damp ground, lays itself
back down, quiet, like snow, but
without snow's brilliance,
its elegance, its crackling shine.

Clouds clear. In the sky
a sliver of a silver moon
Venus chasing, the moon tilted
like a boat, towing a star.

A Cat Sits Under the Moon

A man sings exuberantly in Spanish
up on the roof across the street.

I have died at least once
but I keep talking.

The world as I know it doesn't exist.
A swimming pool takes up the old yard
filled once with the blue of delphiniums
and the red of roses; and a plum tree dropped
its little bitter fruit.

I have died at least once
but I keep talking.

Looking through pictures I've saved:
a woman with a gaping hole
where her heart should be, a stream
gushing out of it.

I have died at least once
but I keep talking.

Another woman cut from a newspaper
leans out a window, elbows on the sill,
looks to the right "in the soft light of Italy."

I have died at least once
but I keep talking.

And a cat sits under the moon.

He and She

He made a plane, the kind
you shave wood with, from epoxy
and razor blades.

He's trying to make
a two-stringed guitar, taking the plane
to the wood until it's straight

as the neck of a swan, outstretched.

***

New little green leaves shine
from the candelabra
of the Rose of Sharon. Can you

see it, the candelabra of mostly
bare branches?

This branch stands up and cries
Look! It's another spring.

And she says,
"Why do you write about trees
and flowers?"

Suzanne, they are constant, true
and alive.

Acknowledgements

Grateful acknowledgement to the editors of the following publications in which these poems first appeared:

Avatar: "Hummingbird," "The Language of Walking," "The Orient Express," "Snapshots," and "Warrior Woman"
Blue Heron Review: "The Last Rose of Summer"
Convergence: "Dinosaur Tail," "In the Sandwich Shop," and "Spring and Fall"
Caesura: "In Defense of Plants"
Ekphrasis: "On a Painting by John Meyer"
Fragments, an Internet collaboration of poets, artists and musicians: "Agapanthus, or Lily of the Nile," "Feathers" (originally published as "After Stanley Plumly"), "Frankenstein's Monster Looks Back," and "Go with Me, God of the Dogwood"
Innisfree Poetry Journal: "Curtains," "Obsession with the Dogwood," and "Smoke"
Montucky Review: "Eavesdropper"
Poetry Breakfast: "The Woman Who Fed the Doves"
Peacock Journal: "A Cat Sits Under the Moon," "November," and "This is the Place"
Turtle Island Quarterly: "A Moment in April" and "Ciao"
Women Artists Date Book 2013: "Who Is the Bear?"
WTF: "A Night Out," "If You Are a Prisoner," and "Roses in March"

About the Author

Jane Blue has been published widely both in print and online, including anthologies, books, and chapbooks. She is the author of four previous books of poetry and one memoir. Recent publications includes *Avatar*, *Panoplyzine*, *Poetry Breakfast*, *Innisfree Poetry Journal*, *Turtle Island Quarterly*, and the anthology *Unrequited Love*. Her poems have also appeared in, among others, *Antigonish*, *The Chattahoochee Review*, *The Montserrat Review*, *Poetry International*, *The Louisville Review*, *Spoon River Poetry Review*, and *Salt Hill*. She was born and raised in Berkeley, CA and currently lives in Sacramento, CA.